How Your
"Financial Planner"
Failed You

Retirement Income
Planning Essentials

Michael Mansfield, MBA-FP, CFP®

This document discusses general concepts for retirement planning, and is not intended to provide tax or legal advice. Individuals are urged to consult with their tax and legal professionals regarding these issues. This handbook should ensure that clients understand a) that annuities and some of their features have costs associated with them; b) that income received from annuities is taxable; and c) that annuities used to fund IRAs do not afford any additional measure of tax deferral for the IRA owner.

Printed in the United States of America

First Printing, 2017

Michael J. Mansfield
The Lynd Group
801 South Victoria Ave., Suite 105
Ventura, CA. 93003 (805)500-7035

ISBN-13: 978-1548094836
ISBN-10: 1548094838

Table of Contents

ACKNOWLEDGEMENT

As a child, I remember looking at the Family Circus cartoons in the newspaper. How funny it seemed that a family could be so big and so busy. As an adult, perhaps the family circus has come to life. There are so many activities between work and family life that pull me in so many directions. I wrote this book because I have a passion for what I do. But these projects are sacrifices for other areas of my life.

I want to thank my beautiful wife and wonderful daughters for all of the love, support and patience they lend me to pursue such endeavours. I love my family very much. My mother, Debra, is my business partner. I owe her a huge debt of gratitude for all of the efforts she makes to assure our business and clients never, for a moment, go unattended. As for my father, he planted the seeds of my path when I was a young boy. His own work ethic has always been an example of accomplishment. It is a real blessing to have my family support.

INTRODUCTION

Studies show that on average 10,000 baby boomers are retiring daily. This creates a need and demand on the financial services industry to adopt effective methods of helping boomers transition into the distribution phase of their lives. Being that we shape opinions about money, investing and financial goals throughout our working years, the challenge of this transition to retirement can be burdensome. Oftentimes, these acquired attitudes can contradict the needed solutions to create a successful retirement.

In service of this philosophy, Michael has developed this book as a proprietary retirement system; which allows clients to truly define their goals, map out their future, and properly track their progress. At its core, this system is a tool to build recommendations for clients: showing them where financial inefficiencies exist, clearly depicting the relationship between returns and risk, and creating holistic and purposeful financial strategies to help clients reach their goals. Ultimately, Michael hopes to provide a tangible and individualized palette of options that clients can use to build the retirement plan they desire.

Michael's hope is that you read this book and gain a basic understanding in shaping the big picture of your retirement income plan. Concepts in this book are designed as an overview to establish the process and expectations you should have when working with your financial professional.

1

RETIREMENT INCOME PLANNING:
A TEST IN ORGANIZING

The financial services industry is ripe with "financial planners" who don't actually plan anything. Let's illustrate:

Do your investments remind you of a monster truck, a Smart Car, or a Toyota Camry?

When designing a vehicle, we would probably all agree that the overall shape and styling are core concerns when working toward the design goal. So how do you actually design a vehicle? Does the engineer typically start by shaping wheels and tires first? Not likely! They get a blank block of clay and they use tools to mold the desired look; they form the big picture.

It would be considered that the normal vehicle (the middle class) typically needs similar design features. The shape of the vehicle needs to be aerodynamic and efficient. Once the overall vehicle design is properly shaped, it is then time to refine details such as the appropriate wheels and trim. Car designers know that considerations of design will always include safety features and comfort considerations.

Now we need to talk about the "retirement vehicle." Interestingly enough, the same application of creating a car goes into the fundamentals of designing and establishing a proper retirement income plan.

So really, the point is to first organize the big picture of your retirement goals. Once you have designed the big picture of what your cash flows, expenses and desired income looks like, then you have a template for shaping the clay of your retirement.

Going back to the analogy, I consider the Toyota Camry as an efficient, reasonable and successful looking retirement vehicle. A Toyota Camry gets good gas mileage, has comfortable leg room, is reliable, dependable, and can provide any commuter with reasonable transportation. To be clear, this image should be the core basis for how we should view our retirement income goals.

> **REMEMBER** - the Camry was shaped from a blank block of clay. You need to consider your retirement tools as the same block of clay.

With investing, it is a typical mistake to first purchase investments; then figure out how that investment will fit into your retirement income goals. This common mistake can be compared to designing the wheels before the car!

This is the same example of why we do not pick investments first in retirement income planning. Rather, we establish our cash flows, then shape the big picture of what we need to be comfortable (our expenses).

For example, if you take your 401(k) and you throw a ton of money into some giant investment (without a plan), maybe you just accidentally put monster truck tires on your Toyota Camry. Picture that for a second. How would the vehicle look and function? You might still be able to drive down the road with your monster truck tires; but let's be fair, your gas mileage stinks, and your retirement vehicle does not function correctly. Simply put, you lack balance and efficiency with your design.

On the other hand, if you allow some financial professional to take a small little tiny account from you (the industry calls this the low hanging fruit), and open up an account, with no big picture purpose of how it affects your plans, maybe you accidentally just put Smart Car tires on your Toyota Camry.

Now take a moment to picture that. Once again, you might drive down the road but your retirement vehicle will not function as well as a Toyota Camry would; will it?

If you are not careful, you might end up with a bunch of accounts with undefined goals. What a mess. Your retirement vehicle is looking like a lemon.

This analogy highlights the fundamental failure of "financial planners" actually planning anything prior to selling you products. To re-enforce this theme, here is a scary statistic:

"Less than 14% of baby-boomers have any type of written retirement strategy."
-Transamerica Center for Retirement Studies

If you are a part of the over 86% of boomers that own investments and financial products, yet have no idea how to use them in retirement income planning, how scary!

So hopefully, this analogy offers some basic perspective to how you and a financial professional should approach creating a retirement income plan.

You have to be vigilant about the size of the tires you put on your retirement vehicle. You have to ask core questions to your financial professional when moving money and establishing new accounts:

- Why are you recommending this type of investment vehicle?
- Why do you feel this amount of money, in this new investment, with help my overall retirement and income goals?
- If this new account is for income planning, when & how will I access it?

When considering retirement income planning, the hardest part is not picking the correct investment vehicles, but rather defining why you even need a particular investment.

- What is the value of a particular investment for your situation?
- Why do you need that amount of money in that type of investment?
- What is the end goal of investing and utilizing that asset class?

> **REMEMBER** - It is not difficult to pick investments. But, it is hard to assign the purpose of the investment. Planning takes effort!

To review, if you allow a financial professional to put too much money in one particular type of investment, maybe that investment suddenly put monster truck tires on your retirement vehicle. It is likely too big, too large and too dangerous; and the problem is there is no **purpose** on how this investment is going to fit into your effective and efficient retirement income plans.

At the same time, what is the purpose of allowing a financial professional to rollover your small account into some other small investment? How is that investment, with that amount of money going to help your retirement income plans? It is likely that you just ended up with Smart Car tires on your retirement vehicle.

You have to assign purpose to why you are investing the amounts of money you are investing in specific accounts. This is the only way to formulate and effectively create a proper retirement income plan.

So back to my question:

Do your investments remind you of a monster truck, a smart car, or a Toyota Camry?

These three vehicles certainly highlight the fundamental challenges with proper retirement income and cash flow planning. The analogy of these three cars really comes from the nature of investment advice. If you are working with an insurance agent or stockbroker, and getting "suitability" level investment ideas (chapter 9 will cover this better), then it is likely that one of your investments looks like either a monster truck or Smart Car.

The purpose of this book is to help you organize your goals in a manner that you can affectively deploy throughout retirement:

- **What do you want your retirement to look like?**
- **What do you want your retirement income to feel like?**

Point being, if you equate your retirement cash flow to a car, you probably want it to look like a Toyota Camry. Retirement is supposed to be that efficient vehicle. It is supposed to offer us a very reasonable way to get from point A to point B; without a lot of drama and without needing a lot of repairs. You need a retirement plan that gives you good gas mileage. You need your target retirement to offer you a certain level of protection.

If your assets have been organized to look like a monster truck or Smart Car, you probably are not achieving the needed goals with your retirement vehicle.

The best way to start designing your vehicle is to consider the source of advice. Are you working with a fiduciary? Now times are changing, the Department of Labor has mandated that any stockbroker, insurance agent or anyone that deals with retirement accounts is now a "fiduciary." This becomes a challenge for our industry. You have to work with an expert that understands and specializes in retirement cash flow income planning.

Do your homework. Research your financial professional and ask these minimum questions:

- Do they have experience?
- What type of securities/insurance license do they carry?
- Do they have formal financial education?
- Do they go above and beyond the basics by getting certifications and designations?
- What have they done in the industry to show their commitment to their profession?
- What makes them an expert with what you need?
    - Distribution phase income planning!

REMEMBER – You only have one life's savings, and you only have one chance to do retirement correctly.

2

ESTABLISHING THE INCOME GAP

At this point we have determined that your retirement probably looks like some type of wonky car with monster truck tires. We have also discussed the importance of formulating a big picture plan, before picking your retirement investments. Now it is time to begin shaping your retirement plans. This chapter will highlight the overview of income and cash flow planning.

So, what is the first step in retirement income planning? The answer is simple, we have to establish your **INCOME GAP**.

The core of retirement income planning is really about "paychecks." Consider this, for your whole life you worked very hard to bring home a paycheck. You went out the front door, you applied energy and effort, and as a result you received that paycheck. This paycheck was then designed to pay for your lifestyle, pay your bills, save for retirement, provide for other people, and so much more.

Well the simplicity of retirement is about recreating that same paycheck. The fundamental difference being that in retirement, you will not be going out the front door each day in order to earn your paycheck. This change as you enter retirement is what I call the "retirement income cliff."

The concept of establishing the income gap is an exercise in organizing, the above mentioned, paychecks. In order to establish your income gap, we have to take an organized approach to understanding the tools and resources you have accumulated for your retirement plans.

First, you have to understand and maximize your "magic money." The magic money is the most important kind, because it is not coming out of your pocket! It is coming in from the world. **This is Social Security, pensions and other external cash flows.**

Often times these cash flows are very powerful, because they come with some type of cost-of-living adjustment (COLA). But remember, paychecks coming in from the world are very different than paychecks coming in from your investments. Paychecks created from your investments are really just you living on your savings.

You want to try to reserve your savings as much as possible. That is why it is imperative that you maximize and put great consideration into your external cash flow sources or magic money.

Step 1 - $$ Coming In ??

Most people are going to have access to Social Security. Social Security comes in many forms. This can be your own benefit, spousal benefits, ex-spouse benefits, survivorship benefits, or some type of dependent benefit. Additionally, if you are married, your spouse will also have access to the same type of benefits (Chapter 3 will go into better detail). In most retirement cash flow planning situations, Social Security maximization should and will be the cornerstone of your retirement income plans.

> **REMEMBER** – Social Security maximization is the very first step that you want to take when building a retirement income plan.

Next, you look at maximizing any other external income sources. If you have a pension, you have to consider the source of the pension. Pensions from private employers typically mean you were also funding Social Security taxes. Therefore, there are normally no penalties or challenges with taking a private employer pension and Social Security benefits.

If you have a pension from some type of government related work, there could be penalties to your Social Security. It is important that you spend the time properly understanding the nature of your pension. Additionally, you need to understand the potential payout and survivorship options of this paycheck (Chapter 4 will go into detail on pension sources).

> **REMEMBER** – The correct financial professional should be able to help navigate and organize your external income sources!

Additionally, you need to review paychecks coming from things such as income/rental properties. Typically, real estate investments can be considered an external cash flow. This is because real estate does not have the same characteristics as pulling money out of an individual investment account.

Overall, the goal is to maximize Social Security, maximize pensions and maximize any external cash flows. You then have to stress test these cash flows; which becomes rather morbid. What happens to the cash flows if "spouse A" passes away, versus what happens to the cash flows if "spouse B" passes away?

There is a huge amount of consideration that goes into mapping out and maximizing these external cash flows, which is once again is why we call it the magic money! Step 1 summary:

1. $$ Coming In ??
Social Security
Pensions
Rentals
Other external Income

Step 2 - $$ Going Out ??

The second part of establishing the income gap is perhaps the most challenging part. This is the area where you have to emphasize and focus on your expenses. With expense planning, this can be very challenging. That is because expenses are living and breathing. They are constantly changing, they are constantly increasing, and they are constantly decreasing. You have to spend time understanding what your current fixed expenses are and build an allocation for your variable expenses above and beyond the fixed.

Some components of organizing expenses are simple. For example, if you have a mortgage, you know how long you

13

will have that mortgage for, and you also know what those fixed payments look like. The same goes for expense items such as property taxes and property insurance.

Additionally, if you are of Medicare age, you should have a very strong understanding of what Medicare costs are; including the premium cost-of-living adjustments.

As you approach **variable expenses**, this is where the challenges arise for many people in the planning process. It becomes important to understand things such as your dining-out habits, your entertainment habits, your traveling habits, and the associated risks that arise from health events.

Overall, you need to spend time examining and defining your expenses and your spending habits. This is something that needs to be regularly updated in the proper retirement income plan. Step 2 summary:

2. $$ Going Out ??
Home
Medical
Personal
Variable Expenses

Step 3 – Solve the Income Gap!

The third step starts with some very basic math. Once you have sorted out what your monthly paychecks are from your external cash flows, you take that number and you subtract whatever you came up with in your expense column. This is going to establish the baseline for what is known as your **INCOME GAP**.

For example, if you have $7,000 a month coming in paychecks from external sources, and you are spending $10,000 a month on average, then you have a monthly income deficiency of -$3,000 (this is your income gap). Step 3 & income gap calculation summary:

1. $$ Coming in?	2. $$ Going Out?	3. Income Gap!
Social Security	Home	401k
Pensions	Medical	IRA
Rentals	Personal	Bank
Other Income	Variable Expenses	Other Savings
i.e. $7,000/mo.	i.e. $10,000/mo.	i.e. -$3,000/mo.

This template gives you a substantial piece of information when it comes to organizing and planning retirement income cash flows needs. Additionally, all of the information you have brought together for this analysis is shaping your efficient retirement vehicle.

With this basic understanding of your retirement cash flow, you can start organizing your investments; in a manner that allows you and your financial professional to solve your income gap.

Be aware that identifying your income gap can be a concerning realization. That is because income gap solutions come from backfilling the needed income with your savings. Perhaps, your income gap is more than you thought it might be. For example, maybe you thought you would only need $3,000 a month in retirement from your investments and you really need $5,000 a month. That can feel overwhelming.

Fortunately, understanding this information allows you to consider the situation. If it is determined that you do not have enough assets to support your income gap, there are a number of potential considerations. This would include:

- **Do you need to work longer?**
- **Do you need to save more?**
- **Do you need to spend less?**

All of these questions have very real and very separate impacts on your overall goals with planning your retirement and establishing your retirement income.

Certainly, you can see the importance of proactive planning in this area. That is because, if you do have some of these challenges with income gap planning, having the time to adjust and make corrective decisions can be invaluable.

As mentioned, from the Transamerica study in Chapter 1, most baby-boomers do not even have this level of planning organized for their retirement income plans. So, what are "financial planners" actually planning?

The chapter 2 overview of "solving your income gap" serves as an oversimplified understanding of cash flow analysis. Unfortunately, real-world situations are not this clean and concise. These real-world considerations bring in many more dynamics to be considered.

For example:

- How would pension survivorship options impact your cash flow analysis?
- What happens to Social Security at the death of the first spouse?
- How will unforeseen expenses impact your income gap and distribution plan?
- How can life expectancies impact the income gap?

All of these points need to be considered in a much more detailed cash flow analysis. The hope is, this chapter gives you the simplicity of the general tools that would be considered when formulating a proper retirement income cash flow analysis.

Additionally, it is imperative that we factor in general long-term considerations. Primarily this would include things like inflation and taxes. Depending on how your assets are organized you should also consider varying ranges of tax exposure. This is highlighted by evaluating the idea of pulling money out of a pre-tax or after-tax account at any given time.

Inflation will certainly impact and increase the necessity of monthly income spending habits. At the same time, the effects of taxes and inflation could be offset by paying off debt, such as mortgages, and reducing overall expenses.

REMEMBER - The worst thing you can do is plan all of this on the day of your retirement.

Consider the theme of Chapter 2; have you taken the time with your financial planner to properly outline these details? Or are they failing you?

As you move though this book, my goal to build off of the previous chapters and help you refine a solid understanding of retirement income planning:

Chapters 3 & 4 are designed to offer you additional depth to the first step of income gap planning; establishing and organizing external paychecks / cash flows.

Chapter 5 will discuss additional considerations for step two of income gap planning; organizing your expenses.

Chapter 6 & 7 will offer insight into step three of the income gap planning; how you use your actual assets to solve for income.

Chapter 8 pulls in additional items that should be considered when creating a proper retirement income plan.

Chapter 9 offers more detailed guidance on financial professionals and the key characterizes you should look for when hiring one to guide you on your life savings.

Chapter 10 summarizes my firms value proposition for your consideration as you approach your own retirement income planning.

3

SOCIAL SECURITY

Now we are going to focus on the first step of establishing the income gap. Social Security is the cornerstone of retirement income planning. So, it is a great place to start!

If you are like most Americans, Social Security is or will be an important part of your retirement income and one that you should know how to properly manage. As a first step in creating your income plan, a financial professional will take a look at your Social Security benefit options. Social Security is the foundation of income planning for anyone who is about to retire and is a reliable paycheck source for your income plan.

Like most retirees, you rely on a Social Security benefit to form the foundation of your retirement plan: the monthly benefit check provides you with a crucial and guaranteed stream of retirement income.

However, despite how many Americans rely on their Social Security benefits to contribute to their retirement income, most people do not fully understand how it operates, which can cause them to make costly mistakes.

For example, had you waited to file for Social Security, your monthly benefit could have been higher, which would have meant less money had to be pulled from your nest egg to contribute to your desired income. Instead, that money could have been put to work for other uses. Ultimately, your Social Security benefit is a crucial tool in your retirement toolbox but it will only be as effective as you know how to use it.

One of the most important things to glean from this chapter, for almost all intents and purposes, you cannot change your Social Security benefit. Once you file for Social Security and begin collecting your monthly benefit, you are permanently locked into that amount.

Consequently, it is vital that you take the time to consider all your options and only file for Social Security when you are positive you are doing so in the right way and at the right time. That said, however, there is one exception to this rule, although it is supremely difficult to take advantage of it: if you have taken less than 12 months of payment and repay all the benefit checks you receive, you can defer filing and reapply later, when your benefit could be potentially higher.

> **REMEMBER** – You really only have one chance to do Social Security correctly.

While there is clearly much more to filing for your Social Security benefit than just filling out the correct paperwork, many people do not understand this.

As the facts below illustrate, the majority of Americans depend on Social Security, but few know how to do so in the most effective way:

- **When you receive a paycheck from your employer, you pay into Social Security**
- **6.2% of your salary is paid by you and 6.2% is paid by your employer**
- **40 credits are needed to be eligible to receive benefits**
  - 1 credit for every $1,300 made annually
  - Maximum 4 credits per year
- **Highest 35 years of earnings are used to determine your Social Security benefit**
  - If you work less than 35 years, the missing years are counted as zero

- 2017 average Social Security benefit is $1,360
- Maximum monthly benefit for 2017 is $2,687
- Maximum taxable income is $127,200

1.   https://www.ssa.gov/pubs/EN-05-10003.pdf
2.   https://www.ssa.gov/pubs/EN-05-10072.pdf
3.   https://www.ssa.gov/pubs/EN-05-10070.pdf

When it comes time for you to cash in on your Social Security benefit, you will have many options and choices. Social Security is a massive government program that manages retirement benefits for millions of people. Experts spend their entire careers understanding and analyzing it.

Luckily, you do not have to understand all of the intricacies of Social Security to maximize its advantages. You simply need to know the best way to manage your Social Security benefit. You need to know exactly what to do to get the most from your Social Security benefit and when to do it. Taking the time to create a roadmap for your Social Security strategy will help ensure that you are able to exact your maximum benefit and efficiently coordinate it with the rest of your retirement plan.

There are many aspects of Social Security that you have no control over. You do not control how much you put into it, and you do not control what it is invested in or how the government manages it. However, you do control when and how you file for benefits.

The real question about Social Security that you need to answer is:

"When should I start taking Social Security?"

While this is the all-important question, there are a couple of key pieces of information you need to track down first.

Before we get into a few calculations and strategies that can make all the difference, let's start by covering the basic information about Social Security which should give you an idea of where you stand. Just as the foundation of a house creates the stable platform for the rest of the framework to rest upon, your Social Security benefit is an important part of your overall retirement plan. The purpose of the information that follows is not to give an exhaustive explanation of how Social Security works, but to give you some tools and questions to start understanding how Social Security affects your retirement and how you can prepare for it.

Let's start with eligibility.

Eligibility. Understanding how and when you are eligible for Social Security benefits will help clarify what to expect when the time comes to claim your benefits.

To receive retirement benefits from Social Security, you must earn eligibility. In almost all cases, Americans born after 1929 must earn 40 quarters of credit to be eligible to draw their Social Security retirement benefit. In 2017, a Social Security credit represents $1,300 earned in a calendar quarter. The number changes as it is indexed each year, but not drastically. Four quarters of credit is the maximum number that can be earned each year. In 2017, an American would have had to earn at least $5,200 to accumulate four credits.

In order to qualify for retirement benefits, you must have earned a minimum number of credits. Additionally, if you are at least 62 years old and have been married to a recipient of Social Security benefits for at least 12 months, you can choose to receive Spousal Benefits.

Although 40 is the minimum number of credits required to begin drawing benefits, it is important to know that once you claim your Social Security benefit, there is no going back. Although there may be cost of living adjustments made, you are locked into that base benefit amount forever.

Primary Insurance Amount. You can think of your Primary Insurance Amount (PIA) like a ripening fruit. It represents the amount of your Social Security benefit at your Full Retirement Age (FRA). Your benefit becomes fully ripe at your FRA, and will neither reduce nor increase due to early or delayed retirement options. If you opt to take benefits before your FRA, however, your monthly benefit will be less than your PIA. You will essentially be picking an unripened fruit. On the one hand, waiting until after your FRA to access your benefits will increase your benefit beyond your PIA. On the other hand, you don't want the fruit to overripen, because every month you wait is one less check you get from the government.

Full Retirement Age. Your FRA is an important figure for anyone who is planning to rely on Social Security benefits in their retirement. Depending on when you were born, there is a specific age at which you will attain FRA. Your FRA is dictated by your year of birth and is the age at which you can begin your full monthly benefit. Your FRA is important because it is half of the equation used to calculate your Social Security benefit. The other half of the equation is based on when you start taking benefits.

When Social Security was initially set up, the FRA was age 65, and it still is for people born before 1938. But as time has passed, the age for receiving full retirement benefits has increased. If you were born between 1938 and 1960, your full retirement age is somewhere on a sliding scale between 65 and 67. Anyone born in 1960 or later will now have to wait until age 67 for full benefits.

Increasing the FRA has helped the government reduce the cost of the Social Security program, which pays out more than a half trillion dollars to beneficiaries every year!

While you can begin collecting benefits as early as age 62, the amount you receive as a monthly benefit will be less than it would be if you wait until you reached your FRA or surpass your FRA. You can also delay receiving benefits up to age 70, in which case your benefits will be higher than your PIA for the rest of your life.

Year of Birth	Full Retirement Age
1937 or earlier	65
1938	65 and 2 months
1939	65 and 4 months
1940	65 and 6 months
1941	65 and 8 months
1942	65 and 10 months
1943 - 1954	**66**
1955	66 and 2 months
1956	66 and 4 months
1957	66 and 6 months
1958	66 and 8 months
1959	66 and 10 months
1960 and later	67

> **REMEMBER** - If you file for Social Security benefits before your FRA, the reduction to your monthly benefit will remain in place for the rest of your life.

Your Social Security income "rolls up" the longer you wait to claim it. Your monthly benefit will continue to increase until you turn 70 years old. But because Social Security is the foundation of most people's retirement, many Americans feel that they don't have control over how or when they receive their benefits. As a matter of fact, only 4 percent of Americans wait until after their FRA to file for benefits! This trend persists, despite the fact that every dollar you increase your Social Security income by means less money you will have to spend from your nest egg to meet your retirement income needs! For many people, creating their Social Security strategy is the most important decision they can make to positively impact their retirement.

Deciding **NOW** or **LATER**: Following the above logic, it makes sense to wait as long as you can to begin receiving your Social Security benefit. However, the answer is not always that simple. Not everyone has the option of waiting. Many people need to rely on Social Security on day one of their retirement. In fact, nearly 50 percent of 62-year-old Americans file for Social Security benefits. Why is this number so high? Some might need the income. Others might be in poor health and do not feel they will live long enough to make FRA worthwhile for themselves or their families. It is also possible, however, that the majority of folks taking an early benefit at age 62 are simply under-informed about Social Security. Perhaps they make this major decision based on rumors and emotion.

Consider Filing Immediately if You:
- **Find your job is unbearable.**
- **Are willing to sacrifice retirement income.**
- **Are not healthy and need a reliable source of income.**

Consider Delaying Your Benefit if You:
- **Want to maximize your retirement income.**
- **Want to increase retirement benefits for your spouse.**
- **Are still working and like it.**
- **Are healthy and willing / able to wait to file.**

So, if you decide to wait, how long should you wait? Lots of people can put it off for a few years, but not everyone can wait until they are 70 years old. Your individual circumstances may be able to help you determine when you should begin taking Social Security. If you do the math, you will quickly see that between ages 62 and 70, there are 96 months in which you can file for your Social Security benefit. If you take into account those 96 months and the 96 months your spouse could also file for Social Security, the number of different strategies for structuring your benefit, you can easily end up with more than 20,000 different scenarios. It is safe to say this is not the kind of math that most people can easily handle. Each month would result in a different benefit amount. The longer you wait, the higher your monthly benefit amount becomes. Each month you wait, however, is one less month that you receive a Social Security paycheck.

> **REMEMBER** - The goal is to maximize your lifetime benefits.

If you know that every month you wait, your Social Security benefit goes up a little bit, and you also know that every month you wait, you receive one less benefit check, how do you determine where the sweet spot is that maximizes your benefits over your lifetime?

Financial professionals have access to software that will calculate the best year and month for you to file for benefits based on your default life expectancy. You can further customize that information by estimating your life expectancy based on your health, habits and family history. If you can then create an income plan that helps you wait until the target date for you to file for Social Security, you can optimize your retirement income strategy to get the most out of your Social Security benefit.

How can you calculate your life expectancy? Well, you do not know exactly how long you will live, but you have a better idea than the government does. They rely on averages to make their calculations. You have much more personal information about your health, lifestyle and family history than they do. You can use that knowledge to game the system and beat all the other people who are making uninformed decisions by filing early for Social Security (Chapter 8 covers Life Expectancy in better detail).

While you can and should educate yourself about how Social Security works, the reality is you do not need to know a lot of general information about Social Security in order to make choices about your retirement. What you do need to know is exactly what to do to maximize your benefit. Because knowing what you need to do has huge impacts on your retirement!

For most Americans, Social Security is the foundation of income planning for retirement. Social Security benefits represent nearly 40 percent of the income of retirees. For many people, it can represent the largest portion of their retirement income. Not treating your Social Security benefit as an asset and investment tool can lead to sub-optimization of your largest source of retirement income.

Despite the importance of knowing when and how to take your Social Security benefit, many of today's retirees and pre-retirees may know little about the mechanics of Social Security and how they can maximize their benefit.

So, to whom should you turn for advice when making this complex decision? Before you pick up the phone and call Uncle Sam, you should know that the Social Security Administration (SSA) representatives are actually prohibited from giving you election advice! Plus, SSA representatives in general are trained to focus on monthly benefit amounts, not the lifetime income for a family.

The three most common ages that people associate with retirement benefits are 62 (Earliest Eligible Age), 66 (Full Retirement Age), and 70 (age at which monthly maximum benefit is reached). In almost all circumstances, however, none of those three most common ages will give you the maximum lifetime benefit.

Your Social Security options do not stop here, however. There is a plethora of other choices you can make to manipulate your benefit payments.

Other Types of Social Security Benefits:

Retired Worker Benefit. This is the benefit with which most people are familiar. The Retired Worker Benefit is what most people are talking about when they refer to Social Security. It is your benefit based on your earnings and the amount that you have paid into the system over the span of your career.

Spousal Benefit. The Spousal Benefit is available to the spouse of someone who is eligible for Retired Worker Benefits. What if there was a way for your spouse to receive his or her benefit for four years and not lose the chance to get his or her maximum benefit when he or she turns age 70? Many people do not know of this strategy and might be missing out on benefits they have earned.

Survivorship Benefit. When one spouse passes away, the survivor is able to receive the larger of the two benefit amounts. This can be impacted if you have a government pension (see Chapter 4).

File and Suspend. This concept allows for a lower-earning spouse to receive up to 50 percent of the other's PIA amount if both spouses file for benefits at the right time. *-Impacted Bipartisan Budget of 2015*

Restricted Application. A higher-earning spouse may be able to start collecting a spousal benefit on the lower-earning spouse's benefit while allowing their own to continue to grow. *-Impacted Bipartisan Budget of 2015*

Ex-Spouse Benefit. A person can receive benefits as a divorced spouse on a former spouse's Social Security record if he or she was married to the former spouse for at least 10 years, is at least age 62 years old, is unmarried, and is not entitled to a higher Social Security benefit on his or her own record.

Important Questions about Your Social Security Benefit:

1. How can I maximize my lifetime benefit?
2. Who will provide reliable advice for making these decisions
3. Will the Social Security Administration provide me with the advice?

   a. The Social Security Administration cannot provide you with advice or strategies for claiming your benefit. They can give you information about your monthly benefit, but that is it. They also do not have the tools to tell you what your specific best option is. They can accurately answer how the system works, but they cannot advise you on what decision to make as to how and when to file for benefits.

REMEMBER - Work with a financial professional to help you develop the most opportune strategy for filing for Social Security: they have access to computer programs that are capable of pinpointing the exact month and year you should file if you want to get the most out of your benefit.

4

OTHER EXTERNAL INCOME SOURCES

As you have learned so far, Social Security, in and of itself, represents a huge amount of proactive planning prior to implementation. But you also need to consider other income sources and how they might supplement, complement, or conflict with your Social Security plans.

For example, pensions are a fantastic external paycheck coming into your retirement income plans. The nature and make up of these pensions can be dramatically different. There are two major types of pensions:

1. Private employer
2. Government

Initially, and more and more **uncommon**, would be some type of private employer pension. For example, if you worked for the airlines, and they gave you a pension for your many years of service.

Often times these types of private employer pensions allowed the participant to also contribute and pay Social Security taxes during their working years. Essentially, what the participant has created now is two pension sources; their Social Security and their employer's pension (think paychecks!).

Evaluating pensions are not as easy as, "hooray I have some free money coming in." It is imperative to spend a lot of time on an individual cash flow analysis of the pension program. The priority would be to understand:

- What are the potential distribution options of this cash flow?
- Does the private pension offer some type of survivorship option to a spouse or loved one?
- Where would a breakeven analysis establish the best time value of money of taking this type of a pension?
- What is the potential life expectancy and cash flow needs of the household?

All of these items become considerations when establishing how a private employer pension might fit into an overall retirement income plan.

Separately, if you have some type of government style pension, there might be some potential complications with your Social Security. There are a number of government programs:

- Public Employee Retirement System (PERS)
- Federal Employee Retirement System (FERS)
- State Teachers Retirement System (STRS)
- Civil Service Retirement System (CSRS)
- **Local County & Municipality pensions**

When evaluating your government pensions, you need to understand if it would be considered a "non-qualified" pension. Meaning, did you have a pension that you funded with the government entity and that you did not pay into Social Security?

If so, you are likely subject to some very common Social Security provisions. There are two core provisions that can impact your Social Security, when accessing a government pension.

The first one is the **Windfall Elimination Provision (WEP)**. This provision affects you claiming your OWN Social Security benefit, on your own record. Depending on the years of service and the amount of "substantial earnings" that you paid into Social Security would dictate what this, potential penalty, would look like. For 2017, $442.50 is the maximum penalty that the Social Security Administration could assess against your monthly paycheck.

There are many rules to properly identify if you would be subject to this full amount. If you paid into Social Security for 20-30 years, it is possible you would not have the full penalty assessed. The second consideration to years paid in, is the amount you earned in those years. Social Security has minimum earnings thresholds that have to be met (Substantial Earnings) in order to qualify for a penalty reduction. Additionally, the actual amount of your government pension can impact the amount of the penalty.

The second provision to consider is the **Government Pension Offset (GPO)**. This rule says if you have a nonqualified government pension, it would affect any type of SPOUSAL, EX-SPOUSE, SURVIVORSHIP, or WIDOW benefits. Understanding this provision is a bit more complicated. It involves comparing 2/3's of your non-qualified pension against the desired Social Security benefit and dollar for dollar reducing your Social Security paycheck.

> **REMEMBER** – WEP & GPO are challenging to sort out; make sure you find a financial professional that properly understands these rules!

If you have a qualified pension, where you funded the pension and also funded Social Security separately, there could be some minor mitigating Social Security offsets, but in general, you should have access to both Social Security and your government style pension; without the complications of the WEP and GPO.

As you can see, it is imperative, in the retirement income planning process that you understand the nature and make up of your pensions in order to properly assess how these penalties and rules might impact in your income plans.

Perhaps the take away on government pensions is that these rules can be tough to sort out. But it is very important to understand the long-term impact of these provisions on any retirement income plan. Especially, before you are ready to trigger benefits. The last thing you want with retirement income planning are significant last-minute surprises.

> **REMEMBER** - To plan effectively, is to be proactive!

As discussed, you now understand that quite a bit of work goes into understanding your pension sources. It is very important, that the time is spent upfront, on understanding the pensions and understanding the potential conflicts associated with Social Security. It should be obvious how a lack of understanding these items can lead to a failure in your retirement income planning process. But so far, this discussion has only scratched the surface of pension planning for retirement.

Understanding the type and nature of your pension is the first step. The next step is now understanding the pension distributions options.

It is very common for a pension program to offer different types of payouts. For example, this could include a lump sum option, a single life option, and potentially multiple survivorship options for spouses or family members. These items might or might not exist in your pension program, hence the necessity of evaluating the details.

Once you understand the payout options associated with your pension, now you have to analyze and understand how they might complement or complicate your retirement income planning needs.

For example, if you are offered a lump sum option, it would be important to do a breakeven analysis. Simply put, if you took the guaranteed income pension, how many years would you need to collect paychecks in order to pocket the amount of money that the pension company would be willing to pay you upfront in a lump sum?

This is important. Because, if your breakeven is only three years, it would be crazy for you to consider the lump-sum option. On the other hand, if your breakeven is 22 years, there might be some additional analysis required to decide if there are better investment opportunities.

I have found that, typically, employer style pensions come with the word "OR" embedded in their pension offer. Meaning you can have your monthly income OR you can have your lump-sum. But generally, you do not get both. Evaluating these choices can be very impactful on your overall plan.

At the same time, if you had a private pension, which is typically created by taking the lumpsum and purchasing a fixed indexed annuity with guaranteed income rider, then you likely get the "AND" option. This means you have the flexibility of receiving the monthly income AND you also have access to the remaining lump sum if you no longer need monthly income; for example, if your health changes, you could take the funds out of the remaining account value for your own care. Additionally, if you pass away the remaining funds are immediately available your family and beneficiaries.

Oftentimes, by selecting the "AND" options, the monthly guaranteed income will be reduced. This is an important cash flow consideration because you have to weigh less income to much greater assets flexibility. This is a simple thought at the moment, but a very complicated analysis to understand the merits of each decision.

For example – Which do you prefer?

| A. Employer pension offering: |
| $500,000 lump-sum **OR** $2,500/mo. for life |
| B. Private pension offering: |
| $500,000 lump-sum* **AND** $2,000/mo. for life |

*lump-sum reduced by monthly distributions

REMEMBER – Evaluating pensions is complicated and requires in-depth analysis.

The next step is to understand the survivorship options. Income planning should always emphasize the surviving spouse. With that in mind, we are always considering the survivorship options.

Everybody who is in a two-income household has the same universal retirement cash flow problem. That is, you are guaranteed a diminishing income in retirement. When the first spouse dies, you will lose income. At a minimum, you will lose one of the Social Security paychecks. If there are no survivorship options, or reduced survivorship options, on your pension, the surviving spouse's income will be diminished even more.

Additionally, you could potentially lose pension sources depending on the pre-selected survivorship options. Due to this guaranteed diminishing income concern, it is essential to evaluate longevity risk in all cash flow analysis.

Going back to the survivorship options on the pension, you need to understand your choices:

- Will your pension provide 100% of income replacement, 75%, 50%, or some other type of ratio or calculation?
- What do those pension survivorship option reductions look like?

We have to understand how these pension payouts fit into the income plan and complement your social security. Without the proper analysis and understanding of pension choices and selection, you could experience significant income reductions to the survivor of the household.

Separately, an evaluation of the creditworthiness of the pension program is also an important aspect of initial retirement planning:

- How is your employer's financial health and the insurability of the pension?
- Have they used a third-party insurance company to insure your pension?

- Have they tried to reserve for the pension internally?
- What are the potential risks if the company was to go out of business?

Other cash flows:

As we explore external cash flows that will help our retirement income plans, rental properties are also an excellent source of cash flow. An investment property does not offer the same type of investment experience that you might get from taking income out of your brokerage account.

In general, real estate is an illiquid asset, it generates immediate tax benefits, it attempts to give you income without abusing the principal, and generally diversifies away from stock market risk.

So, having a positive cash flow rental property can offer some great potential benefits to any retirement income plan. But you have to always consider the risks! If you plan to expose yourself to third-party risk, meaning having renters, then you need to evaluate your insurance limits. At a minimum have an umbrella policy. You need to make sure that you are managing your risk appropriately.

As a final caveat, there is always the potential of gainful employment in retirement. Typically, you do not want to emphasize working income as a significant source; as you do not know how long it might be available to you. But, some type of part or full-time employment can aid any retirement income plan. The general benefit being, a reduced concern associated with larger investment distributions in the early phases of your retirement.

Gainful employment needs to always be considered with your Social Security plans. Prior to your Full Retirement Age, there are earnings limits that will cause penalties on your Social Security paycheck. These rules need to be understood and evaluated in your income plan.

5

IT'S NOT A BUDGET

In chapter 2, we learned that an essential step in establishing your income gap is to identify and outline your expenses. This, perhaps, is the most critical step in the whole process. That is because it is easy to deceive ourselves on what our actual spending habits look like.

In the past, new clients verbally provided me with a nice round figure; typically, in the first meeting. For example, perhaps you think you need $7,000 a month to be comfortable. Then as an exercise, I send you home with an expense worksheet. This worksheet is designed to outline all of the normal expenses that anyone might be considering.

However, sorting out your expenses can become challenging for you to properly outline and identify these items. That is because there are fundamental difficulties with tracking fixed versus variable expenses. Obviously, knowing your monthly mortgage payment is very different than understanding what your monthly eating habits look like.

An important component of identifying current expenditures, is for you to spend time going through your history of spending. Typically, this would mean a labor-intensive study of evaluating, in general, the last 6 to 12 months of spending habits:

- How much do you spend on gas & food?
- How much do you spend on entertainment?
- How much does it cost to maintain your home and utilities?
- How much are your healthcare and medical services?

REMEMBER – it takes real effort to create an accurate expense worksheet.

Fixed Expenses – Generally, these expenses do not have any significant fluctuations on a monthly/annual basis. This would include things like mortgages and phone bills. Oftentimes, there will be minor adjustments to fixed expenses. For example, perhaps your mortgage company adjusts your monthly payment due to an impound adjustment. Or the phone company has an updated fee structure.

Variable Expenses – These can be the wild cards. This includes expenditures that are having significant swings in monthly/annual cost. Examples of variable expenses are traveling, home repairs, food, and healthcare costs.

It is very important to have a rough idea of these variable expenses. For many retirees, most income in retirement will be fixed. Certainly, there will be some adjustments for inflation, but these adjustments will not, generally, keep up with irresponsible spending habits.

Once you feel you have identified your monthly/annual expenses, it is important to make some adjustments. I personally like the 20+20 rule. Meaning, once you have identified your monthly expenses, add 20% to that number; this accounts for most of the "unknowns" of life. Then add another 20% to that number to account for some type of taxation exposure.

Don't forget the **"20+20 Rule"**

> **REMEMBER** - the idea of expenses is to look at what we are spending to keep the doors of life open. But we also have to pay taxes on top of that!

Once you have identified your expenses, now you need to keep track of them. There are many ways to approach this:

1. You could create a manual expense worksheet inside of Microsoft Excel. This is rather easy to do; but can become labor intensive to maintain.
2. You can go old-school and get the pencil and paper out. Once again, very labor intensive.
3. You can look at budgeting software / applications. These are interesting because they offer data aggregation by linking up bank accounts and credit cards. (see the next page)
4. Otherwise, you can see if your bank offers any budgeting support.

For many people, there are a number of different types of software services that can aid in this process. For example, I personally have chosen to have all of my credit cards and all of my banking at one institution. That is because my bank offers and generates a spending report. This spending report gives me the opportunity to go in and, if needed, re-categorize different expenditures. Then it gives me monthly breakdowns, and annual averages.

Because I use the credit card at the same institution, all of my monthly spending habits on that card are easily and automatically populated into my spending report. This gives me detailed information of how much I am **spending** and how my overall **spending habits** are trending. This becomes an effective tool to track and maintain expenses. Additionally, this type of technology allows you to recall any changes to your regular expenses.

Additionally, you can find many different vendors of software that will attempt to help you aggregate and understand spending habits. For example:

- BillGuard*
- Dollarbird
- Fudget*
- Goodbudget*
- LearnVest*
- Level Money
- Mint
- Mvelopes*
- Penny
- Personal Capital
- Wallaby
- Wally

*Be aware that some of these vendors do charge a fee for service

Retirement income planning and expense planning are considered "living and breathing" items in your life. Meaning, things that are always changing. For example, if you have a mortgage now, it is likely you might not have a mortgage someday. So, it is very important to understand when this mortgage is going to be paid off and how that might positively benefit your overall cash flows. The same considerations exist with healthcare. If you are on private healthcare prior to age 65, possibly your healthcare premiums are more expensive now then they will be when you reach Medicare age. Once again, this is why you need to understand your expenses now; but also spend time projecting future expenses and future goals.

REMEMBER – Expense are living and breathing!

The next component to expense planning is **inflation** considerations. When I graduated high school, I went down to the local Toyota dealership. Though I had no money, it did not stop me from fantasizing about a brand-new Toyota truck. The interesting thing was, back then, you could purchase a fully loaded 4x4 Tacoma for around $20,000. I even remember thinking how impossible that cost was for me. Recently, I was helping a client purchase a Toyota minivan. My curiosity got the best of me, and I walked over to a fully loaded 4x4 Tacoma. I almost fell over with true sticker-shock. The truck was $43,000. Ouch.

REMEMBER – Things get more expensive.

Food, housing, insurance, healthcare, you name it, everything will increase over time. Since the year 2000, inflation has averaged around 2.20% (www.usinflationcalculator.com). It is also easy to look at time periods when inflation was significantly higher and lower. That inflation estimate is also generalized. A real concern would be the rate that healthcare is increasing in cost; well above the average inflation rate. The expectation with baby-boomers needing more and more healthcare and long-term care services will force these costs up significantly over the next 20 years.

The point is, as you evaluate your expenses and desired retirement income, you have to adjust for inflation. Otherwise, in time, your planned cash flow will begin to fail.

> **REMEMBER** - It can be challenging to analyze the impact of inflation on your income needs, without the proper software. If you have the right financial professional, they should have the appropriate resources to run these projections for you.

It is important to create a visual picture of your desired income to cover projected expenses. This is typically done with some type of cash flow software. With the correct program, you be able to see your desired income, adjustments for inflation, and offsets based on expense adjustments.

Example:

- $50,000 income goal

- 2% annual inflation

- $45,000 income goal in year 10, due to paying off mortgage

Years	Income Goal
1	$50,000
2	$51,000
3	$52,020
4	$53,060
5	$54,122
6	$55,204
7	$56,308
8	$57,434
9	$58,583
10	$45,000
11	$45,900
12	$46,818
13	$47,754
14	$48,709
15	$49,684

6

SOLVING THE INCOME GAP

Perhaps the most challenging component of retirement income planning is giving a true and proper assessment of establishing your income gap. It seems to be human nature to rationalize income and spending habits. However, it is important that you really spend the time to analyze and evaluate what your income sources are, how to maximize them, and offset those incomes with true, actual and expected expenses. Once you have done that, then the core concern is how you correctly deal with your income gap.

Your income gap solution is a culmination of all of your life's hard work. As you went through your accumulation phase of life you saved, hopefully, in a number of different asset classes. Perhaps you have a 401(k), IRA's, after-tax investments, real estate, bank accounts, and any other liquid accessible assets.

At this point, you can now understand the outline of how you establish your income gap. Hopefully, you see the value in how this information creates the critical template needed for creating your retirement income plans.

The next step is to create an asset inventory. You cannot develop an income plan until you understand the tools that you have at your disposal. This inventory should include who the account belongs to, value, tax vesting and type of account. This is a very straightforward task to complete and this is always the initial step for every client. Though simple, asset inventorying is invaluable so you do not lose sight on who owns what and understanding the rules for any potential penalties or tax concerns per asset.

Often times, clients do not fully understand their investments. Perhaps you have a 401(k) with a dozen different mutual funds in it:

- **Do you really understand what those mutual funds are?**
- **How do the funds work?**
- **What is the fee structure of your funds?**

It is likely that the answer is "No." To be fair, most financial professionals would not understand any of these items on face value; if they were simply looking at your investment statement.

To create a retirement income plan, you do need to understand the underlying make up and working of your asset classes. The most effective tool that I have found for doing this analysis is through MorningStar.com. Morningstar offers an "X-Ray" feature. This software allows you, or your financial professional, to enter in all of your different investments, weighted by the dollar amount in which you own them, and generate a very objective and comprehensive analysis of your portfolio.

REMEMBER - If you pick a financial professional that focuses on retirement income planning, they should have access to these types of tools for you.

Unfortunately, in my personal practice, I have only had one client in 12 years ever mention that they have seen this type of report/analysis previously. This is a bit scary, because remember, my job is to be a fiduciary and act in your best interest. If I am not objectively analyzing your portfolio, how am I offering you un-biased investment advice? Without the appropriate analysis, I would simply be stating personal opinion. You need the facts!

Everybody has the ability to access the MorningStar.com software. The challenge is, you would have to pay for it, and understand how to use it. It can be a rather complicated application if you do not understand what you are doing. To this point, it is much easier to have the professional do this for you.

Once you have populated the Morningstar X-Ray analysis of your investment portfolio, now you and your financial professional will have a significant amount of data to analyze and absorb.

Over the next few pages, you will see some basic snapshots of some of the data that can be derived from your Morningstar analysis. The core items you can gain from a Morningstar X-Ray analysis would include:

Section 1:

- **Establishing your current risk tolerance of equity and fixed income**
- **Establishing a benchmark as a comparison to your portfolio**
- **Understanding the underlying make up of your equity exposure and fixed income assets:**

Asset Allocation	Portfolio Long	Portfolio Short	Portfolio Net	Bmark Net
Cash	14.24	0.20	14.04	0.00
US Stock	70.36	0.00	70.36	74.33
Non US Stock	0.64	0.00	0.64	0.67
Bond	14.09	0.08	14.01	0.00
Other	1.03	0.08	0.95	0.00
Not Classified	0.00	0.00	0.00	25.00
Total	100.36	0.36	100.00	100.00

Without properly comparing your portfolio to a benchmark, there is no good way for you to objectively understand how your level of risk is actually preforming.

Section 2:

- **Evaluating your percentage weights in different sectors.**
- **Understanding your U.S. and global diversification:**

	Portfolio %	Bmark %		Portfolio %	Bmark %
Defen	**18.37**	**26.33**	**Americas**	**99.17**	**99.11**
Cons Defensive	3.07	9.44	North America	99.14	99.11
Healthcare	13.87	13.74	Central/Latin	0.03	0.00
Utilities	1.43	3.15	**Greater Asia**	**0.27**	**0.47**
Sens	**71.77**	**41.16**	Japan	0.07	0.00
Comm Svcs	1.09	4.18	Australasia	0.02	0.00
Energy	65.99	7.21	Asia Developed	0.09	0.07
Industrials	2.25	10.72	Asia emerging	0.09	0.40
Technology	2.44	19.05	**Greater Europe**	**0.57**	**0.42**
Cycl	**9.85**	**32.51**	United Kingdom	0.12	0.08
Basic Matls	0.83	2.81	Europe Developed	0.39	0.34
Cons Cyclical	1.97	11.21	Europe Emerging	0.01	0.00
Financial Svcs	6.63	16.21	Africa/Middle East	0.05	0.00
Real Estate	0.42	2.28	Not Classified	0.00	0.00

Investing your assets in a number of sectors allows for an initial level of diversification. As you can see above, this portfolio is holding almost 66% of its funds in the "Energy" sector. This should lead you to the conclusion that there is a lack of diversification. Until Morningstar populates this detail, it is likely that you, or your financial professional, were not totally aware the full energy exposure; this certainly rings true if the investments were inside of mutual funds or exchange traded funds.

Section 3:

- **Understanding historical returns compared to a benchmark:**

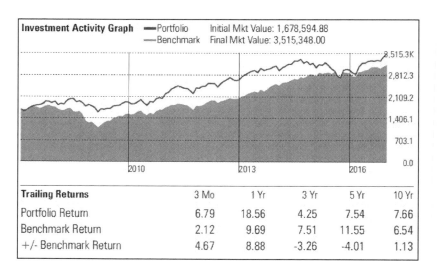

Trailing Returns	3 Mo	1 Yr	3 Yr	5 Yr	10 Yr
Portfolio Return	6.79	18.56	4.25	7.54	7.66
Benchmark Return	2.12	9.69	7.51	11.55	6.54
+/- Benchmark Return	4.67	8.88	-3.26	-4.01	1.13

Comparing your investment returns to a comparable risk portfolio is known as **benchmarking**. Anytime you take risk, investment values will fluctuate. Whether your portfolio is going up or down, it is important to compare that change to the **benchmark**. This allows you, as an investor, to decide if you have taken on investment risk efficiently or inefficiently.

The Morningstar X-Ray analysis will give you time periods, up to 10 years to compare to your benchmark. Depending on how long you have held your investments, will dictate the relevance of this data. Furthermore, historical returns might offer insight to how your portfolio performs in different market cycles.

Oftentimes, anomalies in your returns, compared to the benchmark, are explained via sector diversification or the induvial underlying position.

Section 4:

- **Identifying current yields coming out of the portfolio:**

Portfolio Yield	Yield %
Trailing 12 Month	3.10

Dividends and yield can be a powerful tool when dealing with long-term volatility. In the above picture, the portfolio yield is 3.10%. So, in a given year, if your assets lost -10%, your NET result for the year would be -6.90%. At the same time, if your portfolio increased 10%, you still receive the dividends and your total return would be 13.10%.

Section 5:

- Understanding the credit rating of your fixed income
- Identifying the maturity and duration risk

Credit Quality	% of Bonds
AAA	74.89
AA	3.63
A	9.51
BBB	11.55
BB	0.14
B	0.11
Below B	0.04
NR/NA	0.14
Interest Rate Risk	Portfolio
Maturity	8.30
Duration (total portfolio)	6.00
Avg Credit Quality	AA

Understanding the credit quality of your fixed income bond portfolio is very important. The difference between investment grade and junk bonds can be drastically different with your expected investment experience. Additionally, in an age of low interest rates, the length of the bonds can be significantly impacted by interest rate risk.

Section 6:

Additionally, you will have a good understanding of the statistical measures of your portfolio in comparison to a benchmark. This is likely considered the mathematical "brains" of your portfolio. The core statistical measures to analyze in this report would be:

- **Standard deviation**
- **Mean**
- **Alpha**
- **Beta**

Risk and Return Statistics	3 Yr		5 Yr		10 Yr	
As of Date 12/31/2016	Portfolio	B-mark	Portfolio	B-mark	Portfolio	B-mark
Standard Deviation	11.63	8.01	10.31	7.73	11.52	11.50
Mean	4.25	7.51	7.54	11.55	7.66	6.54
Sharpe Ratio	0.40	0.93	0.75	1.44	0.64	0.55

MPT Statistics	3 Yr	5 Yr	10 Yr
As of Date 12/31/2016			
Alpha	-3.84	-4.18	2.66
Beta	1.15	1.06	0.74
R-squared	62.32	63.65	55.73

As you can see from these six sections from your Morningstar analysis, portfolio analysis is rather overwhelming and likely too complicated for you to tackle on your own. This reinforces the importance of working with a financial professional that specializes in retirement income planning and that use these types of tools as a template to help you make objective and unemotional decisions.

65

Overall, the Morningstar analysis is one of the many building blocks as you evaluate how to solve your income gap. You cannot start to understand how to organize your assets if you do not even understand what you own.

Then, the biggest challenge of a Morningstar X-Ray analysis is trying to decide what to do with the information. For example, if you came to the conclusion that your statistical measures are not efficient, how do you fix that? This, in and of itself, requires additional analysis.

Now that you have a comprehensive understanding of your portfolio, you have to categorize your underlying assets into the types of investments owned. This will, in turn, help you understand which assets can be better utilized for income planning. Initially, you will focus on two core classifications of investments.

First, you have **"AT-RISK"** investments. This will also be called "**Red Money**." Red typically reminds us of some type of danger. For example, when driving, what happens when you see a red light? You realize if you put your head down and barrel through the intersection, you could create a real problem. Obliviously, your At-Risk / Red assets offer an element of risk; there is a general fluctuation in account value. These would include stocks, bonds, mutual funds, exchange traded funds (ETF's), alternative investments, and variable annuities.

Second, we will look at your **"NON-RISK"** asset classes. These will be called your "**Green Money.**" The color green reminds us of safety. Just like the traffic light, you still want to look both ways, but green generally means it is safe to move forward.

REMEMBER – "Non-Risk" does not mean there is no risk to your investment; there is always default risk based on the institution you give your money to. Non-Risk typically means you have some level of stability and principal protection.

Non-Risk assets will include perhaps the most important items, such as Social Security, pensions, checking and savings accounts, bank CDs, short-term and government style bonds, cash value life insurance, fixed annuities and fixed indexed annuities. Red & Green summary:

At-Risk / Red Money	Non-Risk / Green Money
Stocks	Social Security
Mutual Funds	Pensions
Exchange Traded Funds	Bank Accounts
Alternatives	Bank CD's
Bonds*	Bonds*
Private Placements	Cash Value Life Insurance
Variable Annuities	Fixed / Fixed Index Annuities

*There is a large spectrum of risk when investing in bonds

You will notice, that I included Social Security and pensions inside of the Non-Risk category. That is because you need to think about Social Security and pensions as primary assets in your retirement plans.

Think about it, if your Social Security is going to give you $20,000 a year with a cost-of-living adjustment, how much money would you need in an investment in order to generate that type of cash flow without significant risk? It would be a very large number (likely over $700,000). Therefore, you truly need to remember the importance and value of these sources of retirement income.

Next you need to understand how to use the **At-Risk** and **Non-Risk** assets. This is very simple:

- **Non-Risk** assets are used to create income.
- **At-Risk** assets are used to create long-term growth, and hedge our retirement income plan against taxes and inflation.

When establishing your income plan, identified the income gap, created an inventory, completed a portfolio analysis and organized your red and green money, now we can start to identify how much of our assets need to be shifted in or out of the At-risk and Non-Risk categories. All of this is done in order to start generating your desired income at your desired age.

The make-up of how you use Non-risk assets to generate retirement income, should be entrusted to the techniques and strategies of your financial professional; while considering your individual attitudes towards investing.

For example, it is very common to use a fixed indexed annuity with a guaranteed lifetime income benefit. Essentially this creates a private pension. If you saw that you needed $1,000 a month at age 70 in order to solve your income gap, and you are currently 60 years old. It is a straightforward, easy calculation for your financial professional to advise you on how much needs to be invested now in order to generate that amount of income at that age. For example:

Goal: $1,000/mo.* at age 70 (currently age 60)

Solution: Invest $109,142* Now

*Fixed Index Annuity with Income Guarantee
*Any remaining account value passed to beneficiary
*Investment varies with different companies
*Monthly income paid until death
*Single life payout

REMEMBER - Non-Risk assets are used to create income. At-Risk assets are used to create long-term growth, and hedge your retirement income plan against taxes and inflation.

A very common question that I regularly receive from new clients is, "why shouldn't we use our At-Risk investments to generate monthly income." I have a common analogy that I always consider. Think about it like this:

If your Social Security monthly paycheck was tied to the stock market, meaning if the stock market went down, your Social Security paycheck would go down, how would you feel?

In my career, I have never met anybody that has responded that a reduction in their Social Security paycheck (or pension for that matter) would be okay. Simply put, nobody is comfortable with real risk on retirement income sources.

This same risk to your income exists if you want to use the stock market to generate income. If the stock market goes down, and your investment account loses value, don't you still need your monthly income? If you use your At-Risk assets to create income, if the investments lose value, then you are **Reverse Dollar Cost Averaging (RDCA)**. This affect can have a very devastating and detrimental result on your account. Taking monthly retirement income from your At-Risk assets can potentially cause you to lose control of what your monthly income payments remain at.

Let me reinforce this thought:

If you had $100,000 in a Non-Risk investment and you wanted $5,000 a year of income, do you know how many years, at a minimum, that account would be intact?

The answer is YES, the account would be around for at least 20 years; any interest/returns earned would push this account out further than that.

At the same time, if you put $100,000 in an At-Risk investment and you took out $5,000 a year, do you know, at a minimum, how long that account would last?

The answer is a resounding NO. To be fair, the account could go to two directions, right? But the concern is, the account could be diminished quickly if you experience some type of investment decline and you are pulling out as monthly income; imploding and destroying your account.

Conversely, the investment could increase exponentially and the account may never run out of money. Typically, this scenario is less likely; and in retirement you only have a one chance to do this right. Therefore, you cannot make the mistake of hoping to achieve an above optimal stock market performance.

SOLVING THE INCOME GAP

> **REMEMBER** – Retirement income planning uses
> investment techniques for the DISTRIBUTION phase of
> your life. If you use ACCUMULATION phase
> investment techniques, you could have failures in your
> income sources. You need to change your thinking for
> retirement income planning!

Income planning is not as simple as throwing some assets into risky accounts and some assets into conservative accounts. Retirement income planning highlights the necessity for a competent financial professional that specializes in the income retirement distribution phase of life. That is because you are not typically going to shift all of our assets into green money upfront. Commonly, you are going to consider some type of segmentation or bucketing of assets.

A common strategy for segmenting income goals, is to separate your assets into time periods. For example, how much money will you need to get through the next five years, how much will you need for the next 15 years, how much after that?

Due to these segmentations of time, it allows us to assign risk tolerances to your investments. As we learned about income and At-Risk investments, the sooner you need your money the more dangerous it is to have those funds at risk.

For example, if you had $1,000,000 for income planning, and you desired $40,000/year. Segmenting assets COULD look something like this:

Segment*	Amount*	Risk
Years 1-5	$190,000	Conservative
Years 6-9	$130,000	Conservative Growth
Years 10-15	$135,000	Moderate
Years 15-20	$115,000	Moderate Growth
Years 20+	$430,000	Aggressive

*This is overly simplistic asset segmenting. It assumes an average 4% rate of return and no adjustment for inflation.

REMEMBER – if you wanted to retire in 2009, it would have been devastating to have your "income" assets in the stock market during 2008.

The understanding of time horizon is a significant consideration when evaluating Non-Risk, At-Risk, and desired income.

Additionally, there is a cascading effect of shifting assets from At-Risk to Non-Risk accounts, while moving through your retirement segments. This reinforces the idea that investments should always become more conservative at the time horizon shortens towards actually distributing those funds as income.

For example, if you chose to use short-term bonds as your income solution for the first five years of retirement, maybe after two or three years of income distributions you start to shift more money from your At-Risk investments in your Non-Risk investments; in order to assure that you have the cash flow needed after your first five-year segment.

To that point, as you get closer to your "years 20+", you would need to be adjusting the risk exposure as you prepare those assets for potential income.

I imagine this information was just received with a cloud of confusion. Well, it should have been! It is very complicated to properly segment assets in this manner. To complicate it more, try overlaying taxes and inflation. The point is, you need a retirement income planning professional to help you with this process.

Another core consideration is **double duty**!

When analyzing how to deploy assets in a retirement income plan, always consider using asset classes that might offer you double duty. This is done in two ways. You can purchase a particular investment, or use a certain bucket to accomplish multiple retirement goals.

For example, starting at age 70 1/2, the Internal Revenue Service (IRS) requires you to take a specific percentage of your pre-taxed qualified money out each year. This is called a **Required Minimum Distribution (RMD)**. Typically, these rules would impact accounts like 401K's & IRA's.

Well, if you know you need to keep the IRS happy, and you need to satisfy your income gap, then there is strong rationale to use your pre-tax qualified money as a portion of your retirement income solution. This way you are getting two benefits from those pre-taxed income distributions:

1. **You are getting your income!**
2. **You are making the IRS happy!**

On the other hand, if you chose to solve your income gap with other non-qualified assets, you still have to take your Required Minimum Distributions. This could inherently lead to **extra taxation** in that given year; which was not necessary. Hence, double duty!

Another way to look for double or even triple duty on your assets is considering life insurance as an asset class. Investing money in any type of indexed or cash value life insurance policy can potentially provide you with a number of different features:

- **You could have an investment account that is growing over time and offering an investment return.**

- **You would have a tax-free death benefit.**
  - Typically, this would be much larger than your investment, and received by your beneficiaries if you passed away.
- **Additionally, if you evaluated life insurance correctly, you could even get some type of chronic illness or long-term care benefits.**
  - This means that you would be able to advance your death benefit, while alive, for some of your later-in-life health issues.

In this scenario, we have established one bucket of money that is offering us three very different ways to access your funds. There is also a significant amount of tax efficiency for you and your beneficiaries.

REMEMBER - I stated in chapter 1, it is easy to pick investments, but it is hard to figure out which investments are truly appropriate, why you actually need them and how much to properly invest. Make sure your financial professional is spending the time building out a retirement income plan that considers all of these choices.

Selecting the correct account for income can be extremely valuable when considering the **Medicare Part B High Income Penalty**. If you show more income then desired, due to poor retirement income planning, you will be especially upset when your Medicare premiums are higher than projected.

For 2017, the base Part B premium is $134/mo. This applies to individuals and married couples. As your **Modified Adjusted Gross Income (MAGI).** increases, the potential of paying more for your Medicare Part B and prescription drug plan increases:

Modified Adjusted Gross Income (MAGI)	Part B monthly premium amount	Prescription drug coverage monthly premium amount
Individuals with a MAGI of $85,000 or less Married couples with a MAGI of $170,000 or less	2017 standard premium= $134.00	Your plan premium
Individuals with a MAGI above $85,000 up to $107,000 Married couples with a MAGI above $170,000 up to $214,000	Standard premium + $53.50	Your plan premium + $13.30
Individuals with a MAGI above $107,000 up to $160,000 Married couples with a MAGI above $214,000 up to $320,000	Standard premium + $133.90	Your plan premium + $34.20
Individuals with a MAGI above $160,000 up to $214,000 Married couples with a MAGI above $320,000 up to $428,000	Standard premium + $214.30	Your plan premium + $55.20
Individuals with a MAGI above $214,000 Married couples with a MAGI above $428,000	Standard premium + $294.60	Your plan premium + $76.20

7

GROWTH, SAFETY, LIQUIDITY – PICK 2

So far, I have outlined the big picture of retirement income planning. To this point, you should be able to identify your external cash flows, evaluate your expenses and formulate a baseline income gap. Additionally, you likely have questions about evaluating life events, taxes, inflation and other forces that could potentially impact your plans. This is a great foundation for accomplishing your desired retirement income goals.

In the previous chapter, I discussed the basics of addressing the income gap from an investment standpoint. Now it is important to help you gain a basic understanding of investment structure. This is important because you need to feel confident when evaluating and discussing your distribution phase investment strategies with your financial professional.

Generally, the idea of purchasing an investment vehicle can feel very overwhelming. Commonly, consumers can become paralyzed in the decision-making process; because they lack a reasonable amount of financial literacy. On the other hand, this lack of understanding can lead to giving a financial professional too much trust and purchasing investments that are poorly suited to your income goals.

Additionally, lacking financial understanding allows many consumers to revert to their heuristics and make decisions that lack any individual value. For example, taking financial advice from friends and family could be highly inappropriate, as they do not understand the difference from your situation to their own. Another example would be not purchasing an investment because it charges a fee or commission; rather than identifying the actual merits of that investment recommendation.

The reality is, purchasing investments would be easy if all investment products gave consumers the three core things that they always desire. Think for a second, what would you as an investor like out of picking an investment product:

- **Would you like your investments to have GROWTH potential?** *-yes*

- Would you like your investments to be SAFE and not lose lots of money? *-yes*
- Would you like easy access to your money, and have it LIQUID? *—yes*

My experiences have taught me that most investors would love these three core components with any investment (GROWTH, SAFETY, LIQUIDITY). But let's be fair, if you had low-risk with your investment, its growth rate went straight up to the moon, and you could pull the money out anytime you wanted, wouldn't that be fantastic?

Unfortunately, reality has to set in. When you consider most typical investment options, you get to pick two out of the three core investment desires. So, between growth, safety and liquidity any normal investment is going to offer you two out of the three:

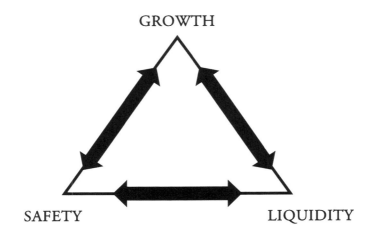

GROWTH & SAFETY

Assume you desire growth and safety from your investment vehicle. Typically, this is going to be some type of insurance product whether that is a fixed or fixed indexed annuity, or some type of cash value life insurance. Insurance, generally, offers principal protection; hence the "safety." Since these insurances follow indexes for earning interest, there is an element of "growth." Commonly, when you invest in insurance products you give up a portion of liquidity for s pre-determined period of time:

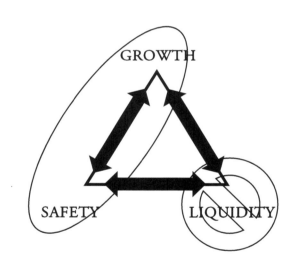

Cash Value Life Insurance
Fixed Annuities
Fixed Index Annuities

GROWTH & LIQUIDITY

If you evaluated investment vehicles that offered growth and liquidity, you would find these choices, generally, lack safety. This would include investments such as stocks, mutual funds and exchange traded funds. The nature of these investments certainly offers the potential of maximum growth. They are also very marketable on an exchange, making them extremely liquid. The challenge being, you give up any safety or stability when you invest here:

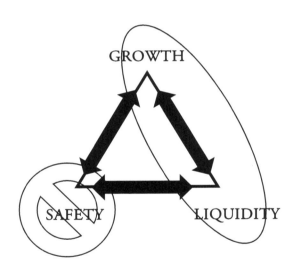

Stocks
Mutual Funds
Exchange Traded Funds

SAFETY & LIQUIDITY

Additionally, if you pursued investments that offered you safety and liquidity, then you will find your growth potential is hindered. In this category, you would include bank accounts, bank CD's, short-term bonds and cash accounts. As you are aware, these asset classes currently offer very little interest growth options:

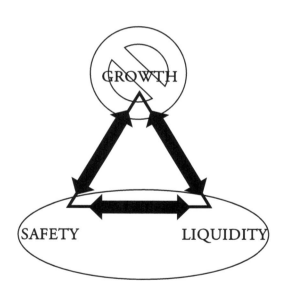

Checking / Savings Accounts
Bank CD's
T-Bill's

As you can see from this exercise, you are always chasing the triangle trying to get all three and only coming up with two. The purpose for discussing this is not to disappoint, but rather help set realistic expectations.

Consider liquidity for example. Often people do not like insurance products because they offer some type of surrender charge, meaning you have limited liquidity for a pre-determined period of time.

Now I find that interesting; let's consider your 401k that you started at aged 30. 401k's have penalties, don't they? In fact, you are penalized on taking money out all the way until you reach age 59 1/2. So, with that bucket of money, that investment vehicle, you have no problem assigning a very long and very high surrender penalty (10%). But, when it comes to retirement income planning, why is it that you have such great concerns about liquidity of an insurance product?

The answer is simple; the problem is the **failure to properly plan**. If you have a properly organized retirement income cash flow plan, then you have the liquid cash for what you need to be comfortable on a monthly/annual basis. You need to properly design the portfolio with elements of liquidity and elements of stability for cash flow. In this scenario, the illiquidity of an insurance product is not nearly as impactful as it would be to the consumer who just threw their monster truck tire amount of money into an insurance product without a plan in place.

Proper retirement income planning will establish a retirement portfolio that offers all the different results that you desire. You will have elements of liquidity that you need. You will have the elements of growth that you need. You have the elements of safety that you need.

To be clear, I feel all retirement income plans need the three core elements of investment makeup:

1. Growth
2. Liquidity
3. Safety

REMEMBER – Always evaluate the pros & cons of all investments, and make decisions based on facts, not emotions.

8

INCOME PLANNING ESSENTIALS

TAXES & OTHER STUFF

To this point, hopefully you have gained a basic understanding of how to begin the shaping of a proper retirement income plan. As mentioned, the tools in this book should help you work with a financial professional to assure your goals are intact. In addition to big picture income planning, there are a number of supportive details to consider. These would include such things as, taxes, life expectancy, risk management, legacy/estate planning and long-term care concerns.

INCOME PLANNING ESSENTIALS

Taxes

Taxes play a starring role in the theater of retirement planning. Everyone is familiar with taxes (you have been paying them your entire working life), but not everyone is familiar with how to make tax planning a part of their retirement strategy.

Taxes are taxes, right? You have to pay them before retirement and you have to pay them during retirement. What's the difference? The truth is that a careful approach to tax planning can help you save money, protect your assets and ensure that your legacy remains intact.

How can a tax form do all that? The answer lies in planning. **Tax planning** and **tax reporting** are two very different things. Most people only report their taxes. March rolls around, people pull out their 1040s or use TurboTax to enter their income and taxable assets, and ship it off to Uncle Sam at the IRS. If you use a CPA to report your taxes, you are essentially paying them to record history. Essentially, most CPA's are basically tax-preparers.

In order to control the effect taxes will have on your overall financial plan you need to make smart, informed, and proactive decisions about taxes. This means you need to work with a Registered Investment Advisor because they are tax-planners. This decision will help to keep you looking forward instead of in the rearview mirror as you enter retirement.

When you retire, you move from the earning and accumulation phase of your life into the asset distribution phase of your life. For most people, this means relying on Social Security, a 401(k), an IRA, or a pension. Wherever you have put your Non-Risk green money for retirement, you are going to start relying on it to provide you with the income that once came in the form of an employer paycheck.

Most of these distributions will be considered income by the IRS and will be taxed as such. There are exceptions to that (not all of your Social Security income is taxed, and income from Roth IRAs is not taxed), but for the most part, your distributions will be subject to income taxes.

Regarding assets that you have in an IRA or a 401(k) plan, when you reach 70 ½ years of age, you will be required to draw a certain amount of money as income each year. That amount depends on your age and the balance in your IRA or 401(k). The amount that you are required to withdraw as income is called a Required Minimum Distribution (RMD).

Why are you required to withdraw money from your own account?

Chances are the money in that account has grown over time, and the government wants to collect taxes on that growth. If you have a large balance in an IRA, there's a chance your RMD could increase your income significantly enough to put you into a higher tax bracket, subjecting you to a higher tax rate.

> **REMEMBER** – Failing to take the correct RMD can result in a 50% IRS tax penalty!

Here is where tax planning can really begin to work strongly in your favor. In the distribution phase of your life, you have a predictable income based on your RMDs, your Social Security benefit and any other income-generating assets you may have. What really impacts you at this stage is how much of that money you keep in your pocket after taxes. Essentially, you will make more money saving on taxes than you will by making more money. If you can reduce your tax burden by 30, 20 or even 10 percent, you earn yourself that much more money by not paying it in taxes.

How do you save money on taxes? By having a plan. In this instance, a financial professional can work with the CPAs at their firm to create a distribution plan that minimizes your taxes and maximizes your annual net income.

So far so good: avoid taxes, maximize your net annual income and have a plan for doing it. When people decide to leverage the experience and resources of a financial professional, they may not be thinking of how distribution planning and tax planning will benefit their portfolios.

Often more exciting, prospects like planning income annuities, investing in the market and structuring investments for growth rule the day. Taxes, however, play a crucial role in retirement planning. Achieving those tax goals requires knowledge of options, foresight and professional guidance.

Finding the path to a good tax plan is not always a simple task. Every tax return you file is different from the one before it because things constantly change. Your expenses change. Planned or unplanned purchases occur. Health care costs, medical bills, an inheritance, property purchases, reaching an age where your RMD kicks in or travel, any number of things can affect how much income you report and how many deductions you take each year.

Preparing for the ever-changing landscape of your financial life requires a tax-diversified portfolio that can be leveraged to balance the incomes, expenditures and deductions that affect you each year. A financial professional will work with you to answer questions like these:

- What does your tax landscape look like?
- Do you have a tax-diversified portfolio robust enough to adapt to your needs?
- Do you have varieties of taxable and non-taxable income planned for retirement?

- Will you be able to maximize your distributions to take advantage of your deductions when you retire?
- Is your portfolio strong enough and tax-diversified enough to adapt to an ever-changing (and usually increasing) tax code?

Life Expectancy

Understanding life expectancy is a key component to retirement income planning. If dying was as simple as knowing the month and year that you were to pass away, it would be extremely easy to properly plan your retirement. The challenge is, life expectancies have been on the rise. A lot of this increase is supported by advances in the medical and technology fields. There are more people than ever living to age 100.

So, the question becomes, what is the appropriate age to plan to? Do we want to use the Social Security life expectancies for you? Likely, they have you passing somewhere before the age of 85. Or do we just use the nice round age 100? When projecting how long your assets need to last, much consideration goes into the nature of the investments you pick and the rate of the drawdowns that you would choose from those investments. This is why understanding life expectancy is very important.

There are some great online tools that can help you understand and estimate your life expectancy. Here are a couple:

www.livingto100.com – This Website is very comprehensive. It has you complete a 40-question quiz about your life and health history.

www.death-clock.org – though the name is whimsical, this is a much simpler life expectancy calculator.

Estimating life expectancy can steer a retirement income plan in many directions. This is especially true for married couples that have two lives to plan around.

> **REMEMBER** - estimating a life expectancy is not a guarantee. You can pass in an accident or linger much longer.

The 4% rule

Historically, identifying an appropriate drawdown rate has been an important component of retirement income planning. Essentially, the 4% rule said that, once retired you could draw 4% of your portfolio value each year without running the risk of going broke.

This was a very popular rule in the early and mid-2000's. After the great recession, interest rates continued their long downward spiral until they bottomed out in 2013. The history of the 4% rule was supported by the fact that bank accounts, CDs, bonds, and other conservative asset classes were offering reasonable rates of return.

As we all know, in the last number of years, interest rates have not offered us those same reasonable returns. Conservative accounts, such as your savings account or bank CD, have not even offered interest rate returns needed for conservative growth or to beat inflation.

Due to this overall decrease in interest rates, it has brought quite a bit of criticism down on the 4% rule. This is exasperated by the previous section where people are having longer life expectancies. The concern is, obviously, if you draw down your assets too quickly, **and you accidentally live too long**, then you could run the risk of going broke.

Morningstar, evaluated the concerns with the 4% rule, in an in-depth study in 2013. The conclusion of their analysis was that a new and more responsible drawdown rate is 2.8%.

Now anybody reading this should look at that number and feel a large amount of concern! Because, in order to generate any income in retirement while only taking 2.8% of your account values means you would need to have a substantial amount of assets in reserve. For many retirees that is unlikely.

Good news, rules (interest rates) change.

The important component of understanding how much you should draw out of your assets is relative to where you are in your retirement plans. If interest rates begin to increase, as they have been in recent history, then you might consider an increase in your drawdown rate.

I personally think, when evaluating the amount of assets to comfortably drawdown, that you should consider a 3% to 5% drawdown rule. What I mean is, your individual drawdown will depend on a number of factors:

- **The size of your income gap.**
- **The older you are, the more likely you are to be able to draw more out.**
  - You can see the importance of evaluating life expectancy in this conversation.
- **The amount of assets you have will have a direct impact on your potential drawdown.**

Savvy financial professionals can lend guidance to beating the drawdown rules. One effective trick to beating the drawdown rules, is purchasing an income producing annuity. This will essentially create a pension with a portion of your assets. The benefit is, if you purchased the correct type of annuity, you are buying "**longevity insurance**."

What I mean is, these insurance products are designed to offer you a guaranteed stream of income for the rest of your life. So, if you are able to get a 6% distribution from investing in an income annuity, and it is guaranteed for the rest of our life, you do not risk that bucket of money running out and leading you to the poorhouse.

This is a powerful strategy when considering the big picture of retirement income planning. But the main challenge is that annuities have a stigma. The attitudes that developed in your accumulation phase of life seem to commonly make us feel offended by the thought of purchasing an annuity. But as we learned in Chapter 7, that in order to get something that you need, it is likely you have to give up something that you do not need as bad. So, it is important to evaluate the merits of insuring your retirement income, while properly weighing the reasons you might not like that type of an investment.

> **REMEMBER** – Annuities have a bad name because of poor sales tactics. It takes significant analysis to property place an annuity in your retirement income vehicle…think monster truck & Smart Car!

One final consideration with this is, understanding that there is no other investable asset class that offers you a similar type of longevity guarantee. If you invest your

Non-Risk green money in short-term bonds, or CDs, the money is gone when it is gone. You have no guarantee of income beyond your account value. There is no longevity insurance.

LEGACY & ESTATE PLANNING

A major component of good retirement housekeeping is ensuring that you have a proper estate plan in place. Estate planning is certainly a nice tool when it comes to planning a legacy for loved ones; but more importantly, estate planning is designed help protect you in your later stages of life. If you were to physically or cognitively decline, you need to make sure that you have the proper paperwork, documentation and people in place to help protect yourself and preserve your wishes.

An important component of estate planning is the common terminology of "avoiding probate." The assumption is, because you have worked so hard your whole life, you do not need the government being your number one beneficiary at your passing. Often times, when estates are poorly planned, the probate process allows the government to stick their finger into your hard work and savings. There are court costs, time costs, public disclosure issues and certainly attorney fees associated with poor estate planning that causes a probate proceeding.

The information here is designed to be a simple overview for two purposes. First and foremost, the most important purpose is making sure that if your health is declining and you cannot care for yourself, resources are in place to do so. Secondly, is simply probate avoidance. If you have a need for more complex estate planning goals, then you will absolutely need to consult with an attorney and focus on advanced levels of estate planning. For example, having significantly high net worth or a special needs child.

With estate planning, you have "above the line" issues and "below the line" issues (the line represents life and death). For me, the above the line issues are the most important ones. This would include things such as a **Financial Power of Attorney (POA)** and an **Advanced Healthcare Directive**. These are the documents that are used to help you, while you are alive, deal with any challenges associated with managing your health and assets.

The below the line issues really exist primarily at the passing of you and your spouse (if you are married). These would include the **Trust** and **Will**. Additionally, there are a couple "wrap up" documents to cover loose ends. These include **HIPAA Authorizations** and **Final Disposition forms**:

Most Important	Financial Power of Attorney
	Advanced Healthcare Directive
Very Important	Trust
	Will
Very Useful	HIPAA Authorization
	Final Disposition

Let me provide a basic outline of these different documents and their purpose:

Financial Power of Attorney - this document allows you to assign an agent, while you are living, to act on your behalf for making financial decisions. This would include financial items, such as:

- Investment accounts
- Real estate
- Banking matters
- Benefits such as Social Security & Medicare
- Pensions

Advanced Healthcare Directive - this document allows you to assign an agent to act on your half regarding healthcare matters. This document specifically allows you to outline your general healthcare wishes. Perhaps, one of the more important components is your **choice to prolong life or not prolong life** when considering life support measures. It is important to realize that the assigned agent's powers supersede your own wishes in this document.

Trust - a living Trust is a document that, in its essence, is designed to assign beneficiary designations to asset classes that do not typically carry beneficiary designations. This core understanding, especially from a probate standpoint, would typically apply to real estate. Perhaps, you own a piece of real estate in our own name or in joint names with a spouse. The question becomes, who does the real estate go to after the death of the listed owners? By vesting your home inside of a Trust, it essentially assigns and creates a legacy plan for that property without the requirement of a probate court.

Will - oftentimes a Will is a catch-all document. Meaning, if you really had a proper estate plan in place, it is likely the Will becomes a rather useless document. That is because if all of your assets are in a Trust or have direct beneficiary designations there is no need for a probate judge to be reading your Will to understand your wishes. At the same time, having a Will in place is a very important component of being preventative with your estate planning. Meaning, if for some reason you failed to properly fund your Trust, the Will would help put things back in the Trust. Additionally, a Will is affective in assigning guardians if you have minor children.

HIPAA Authorization - This document is designed to allow for your agent, and those working on your behalf, to obtain and review your medical records. Sometimes this can be convoluted when only working with an Advanced Healthcare Directive; mainly because a directive allows you to make healthcare decisions, not necessarily giving you access to medical records. For this purpose, it is important to have this standalone authorization. It will allow the listed individuals on the document to obtain whatever medically related records you may desire. This can also become valuable after your passing, if your family is dealing with any bills associated with your medical care.

Final Disposition - This document is designed to give guidance to people that are not overly familiar with your final wishes:

- Would you like to be buried?
- Would you like to be cremated?
- Have you set up any preneed plans at a specific mortuary?
- Do you have a burial plot or specific wishes for the disposition of your ashes?

These questions that can be summarized and answered on this final disposition form. This document is not required when visiting a funeral home in planning someone's passing, rather it is designed to give guidance.

Chapter 8, has covered a number of topics that become essential concerns in the retirement income planning process. Think for a moment, when was the last time your "financial planner" detailed a tax conversation, reviewed potential estate planning holes or evaluating life expectancy in your plans? If not, what are they actually planning?

9

WHO ARE YOU BUYING BAND-AIDS FROM?

UNDERSTANDING FINANCIAL ADVICE

Imagine for a moment that your neighbor is a Band-Aid salesman. This salesman only sells Band-Aids, and nothing else. If you got a cut on your finger, it is likely, you would go see your neighbor and purchase one of those Band-Aids to put on your injury. Doesn't that make sense? Now imagine, what if you were shot in the chest with a gun, would you go ask your neighbor for a Band-Aid once again?

Obviously, the answer is "No!" The point of this analogy is that every situation calls for its own analysis and own considerations. There is no universal Band-Aid that fixes all problems. This is beyond important when evaluating the type of financial professional that you choose to work with.

> **REMEMBER** – How can an insurance agent offer you objective financial planning advice, if they can only offer you insurance solutions?

At this point, I hope you are not feeling overwhelmed. The retirement income planning process, can seem complicated. But, if you are working with a financial professional that specializes in distribution phase income planning, these should be very straightforward thoughts for them to help you analyze and understand.

However, it is important to emphasize the fact that you need to work with the right type of advisor. Just because someone is a financial professional, does not mean they specialize in a specific area of financial services. Are they considered a generalist? Meaning, they help all people with all financial problems and situations? Or are they actually a specialist that is focused on a specific area or niche?

Think of your retirement income plan like a medical problem. If you had cancer are you going to go see your primary care physician? No!

You would do your research and you would find the best oncologist physician that is available to you. You want to get the best professional, accurate and precise help possible. You need to treat your retirement plans with the same attitude and urgency.

In chapter 1, I highlighted the importance of finding a financial professional that can properly help you organize and create a retirement income plan. As mentioned, you need to find a specialist in this area of financial planning.

Now I would like to go into more detail on the different levels of financial professionals and what you should be on the lookout for.

Initially, you need to understand the core distinctions of people that offer "financial planning" advice. This can be broken down into three main categories:

1. **Insurance agents**
2. **Stockbrokers**
3. **Investment advisors**

There is nothing wrong with these different types of financial professionals individually. There is always a necessity for needing an insurance specialist. There always is a necessity for a specialist in stock picking. There is always a necessity for different types of investment advisors.

The challenge is, financial planners tend to hold themselves out above and beyond the scope of their licensing and capability. For example, an insurance agent can only sell insurance. They cannot help you with your stocks, they cannot help you with your 401(k).

So, when you meet with an insurance agent that is holding themselves out as a financial planner, they do not even have the proper licensing to help you understand the full dynamic of investment options based on your individual situation. Actually, by law, they are not allowed to help you with any type of securities investment inside of your 401(k) or investment account.

You would think that the financial services industry has a moral and ethical duty to always do what is best for you. Unfortunately, that theme is a bit clouded. Much of a financial professional's duties falls to what level of standard they are expected to abide by. There are two main standards in the financial services industry that you need to be aware of; **Suitability Standard and Fiduciary Standard**:

Suitability Standard

The lower industry standard to soliciting financial advice is called the **Suitability Standard**. Typically, this would include insurance agents and stockbrokers. They offer products for sale from a range of products carried by the company that the agent or stockbroker represents. They are paid commissions calculated as a percentage of the amount of money invested in that product. Commissions can be created to be paid all upfront, or graded out over a number of years. Commission-based advisors are regulated by the state department of insurance or by Financial Industry Regulatory Authority (FINRA).

As mentioned the insurance agent carries some type of life and health insurance license with their respective state. This type of licensing would allow an insurance agent to sell various life-insurance style products. This would also include fixed and fixed indexed annuities.

Also functioning under that same suitability standard, is the stockbroker. Technically they are called **Registered Representatives (RR)** through a broker dealer. They would likely hold some type of securities license, either a series 6 or series 7. These types of commission based securities transactions would allow them to solicit and sell you different types of stocks, bonds, mutual funds, ETFs, real estate investment trusts, alternative investments, and variable annuities and variable life insurance.

Fiduciary Standard

The higher standard in the industry, is the **Fiduciary Standard**. This means that the investment advisor has to offer the best possible advice to their clients; taking into account the needs of each individual. Typically, investment advisors are paid a fee calculated as a percentage of assets under management. They are regulated by either the Securities Exchange Commission (SEC) or the State Department of Oversight.

Investment Advisor Representatives (IAR) transact and do business through a Registered Investment Advisory firm (RIA). They will typically hold a securities license that is either a series 65 or 66. They still have the ability to sell comparable style investments as a stockbroker, things such as stocks bonds mutual funds and ETFs. The difference is the compensation structure and the expectation of the level of advice that they provide you.

Commonly, it is thought that fee-based fiduciary advisors are a better fit for financial planning services. Meaning, since they did not make a large commission upfront, rather they make smaller fees as they go, they are motivated to make investment decisions that are superior. Essentially, it takes a fee-based advisor many years to generate the same income that the commission advisor makes upfront.

An interesting caveat to these guidelines are the rules for a Certified Financial Planner™. It is common that a CFP® professional will offer both commissioned-based and fee-based investment vehicles. Though these investments technically follow different industry standards, the CFP® Board of Standards mandates that all CFP® professionals operate as a fiduciary at all times. This is very important because you need to know your financial professional is **acting in YOUR best interest at all times.**

> **REMEMBER** – A Certified Financial Planner™ is required to act in your best interest at all times.

To put this in perspective, depending on if your investments are going up or down, you will find a distinct difference between the two industry standards:

FIDUCIARY STANDARD

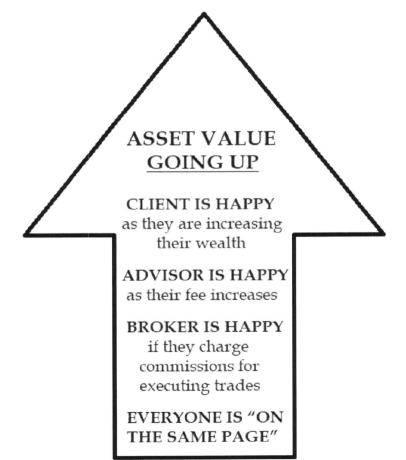

ASSET VALUE GOING UP

CLIENT IS HAPPY
as they are increasing their wealth

ADVISOR IS HAPPY
as their fee increases

BROKER IS HAPPY
if they charge commissions for executing trades

EVERYONE IS "ON THE SAME PAGE"

SUITABILITY STANDARD

ASSET VALUE GOING DOWN

CLIENT IS UNHAPPY
as their wealth is
declining

ADVISOR IS UNHAPPY
as their fee fails

BROKER IS HAPPY
if they charge
commissions for
executing trades

**EVERYONE IS NOT
"ON THE SAME PAGE"**

Did you notice the difference?? When you work with a **fee-based Fiduciary advisor**, they sit on the same side of the table with you. If your investments go down, their income goes down. Nobody wins. I view this as skin in the game! In Fiduciary accounts, the advisor makes the same income whether there is one trade or a thousand trades in the account. Therefore, the reason for account activity is solely to attempt to increase your account value.

10

5 Star Service

Fiduciary Transparency Technology

In Conclusion, thank you for taking the time to educate yourself on retirement income planning. My goal at our firm is to first, demonstrate the principals of this book and second, offering a 5 Star client experience. My value proposition for you consists of these five steps:

1.   Selecting a Financial Services Professional
2.   Fact and Feeling Finding
3.   Planning
4.   Solutions and Executing
5.   Ongoing Relationship

With a focus on retirees, our company uses my Wealth Track Retirement Planning process, which is based on three hallmarks of successful retirement planning: fiduciary, transparency and technology:

FIDUCIARY - Finding a trusted advisor is one of the most important elements of planning your retirement. Providing you with a fiduciary level of service means we are legally bound to always do the right thing for you and your family by only offering solutions that serve your best interest. Our commitment to you as a fiduciary is also an assurance to act with transparency throughout our relationship.

TRANSPARENCY - Our commitment to transparency ensures that each step of our work together is recorded and that every document and report are easily accessible to you. Not only does this allow us to track the evolution of your plan and make any necessary adjustments to it along the way, but you can always see we are acting in your best interest. Our commitment to transparency is visible through a strong foundation of technology.

TECHNOLOGY - Our office utilizes Generational Vault, which is a proprietary online portal accessible through our website. It contains the necessary tools to help make decisions appropriate for you and your retirement. It also serves as the vehicle to document and record our commitment to act as a fiduciary and act with transparency throughout our relationship.

STEP 1 - SELECTING A FINANCIAL SERVICES PROFESSIONAL

Seek a financial services professional and an organization worthy of your trust. Look for one that focuses on putting your needs first with full transparency while utilizing cutting-edge technology to illustrate and execute your ongoing plan, and look for a partner who is committed to achieving your unique financial goals and objectives.

As your financial services professional, I am an investment advisor who is legally bound to provide a fiduciary level of service – which means I am responsible to always act in your best interest.

As your financial services professional, I use a defined process that focuses on transparency to document our interactions while using powerful tools and technology to achieve your financial success.

As your financial services professional, I am committed to an ongoing, long-term relationship with five-star service. Additionally, as your financial services professional, I will provide you with a proprietary technology platform, Generational Vault, so you can have 24/7 access to your financial life. All your accounts, values and important documents such as wills, trusts and financial reports, are all in one place, secure, and readily available.

STEP 2 – FACT AND FEELING FINDING

The second step of New Generation Retirement Planning helps you understand where your assets are currently invested and the amount of risk to which they are exposed. You want your assets secure enough to generate a steady stream of income on the first day of your retirement, but still maintain enough market involvement and growth potential to generate future income.

Our company uses a proprietary software report called **Color of Money Risk Analysis**, which delivers an immediate numerical score and a brief explanation of your risk profile.

This report and your assigned score is designed to help you understand how you feel about potential investment gains and losses so you can appropriately allocate your assets.

Ultimately, how you organize your assets and balance their exposure to risk can have a significant impact on your retirement lifestyle.

Your **Color of Money Risk Analysis** score as well as your answers used to generate your score will be recorded in Generational Vault.

STEP 3 – PLANNING

We believe the assurance of a successful retirement is confidence – it's just easier to execute a plan you believe in. Retirement can be a time of great change and uncertainty, and being confident about your retirement can make all the difference.

In Step Three, we will examine key areas that are fundamental to successful retirement planning, which may vary based on your retirement goals but most commonly begin with an analysis of asset allocation and risk tolerance and include a focus on income planning. Additional consideration and analysis is also offered to include asset maximization, legacy planning and tax strategies.

STEP 4 – SOLUTIONS AND EXECUTING

Any solution we discuss will be based on your facts, feelings, goals, objectives, and the analysis we completed during Step Three: **Planning**. Even years from now, it will be easy to see the process and priorities we used to arrive at a solution.

Our company represents a full spectrum of product providers, which allows us to offer a wide array of financial products. We use independent third-party research to evaluate these products to determine what is in your best interest.

Once a final selection has been made, essential information related to the selection is saved in your **Generational Vault** to ensure proper transparency.

For any potential product solution, you might consider, you will be provided with any relevant company or product brochure, explanation or illustration. It is important that you have all the information you need to understand your options for addressing your financial concerns.

Additionally, we continuously seek to make the process of completing the required paperwork to implement your selected solution as easy as possible through the use of the latest technology. We are pleased to offer efficient solutions, such as pre-populated and electronically-generated forms as well as e-signature capabilities, when appropriate.

Should the **New Generation Retirement Planning** process lead to a recommendation, you should have confidence knowing that every step of the process has been documented through Generational Vault, thus ensuring we have upheld our commitment to act as a fiduciary and act with transparency throughout our relationship.

STEP 5 – ONGOING RELATIONSHIP

There are a number of key resources we implement with all clients in order to establish and reinforce our 5-star service:

GENERATIONAL VAULT - Our Company believes that technology to help you organize, manage and access your financial life is the foundation to successful retirement planning, and we use Generational Vault as well as a proprietary suite of technology accessible through Generational Vault to help deliver on our commitment.

When you partner with our company, Generational Vault provides you immediate access to your financial life, and you will instantly benefit from its power through increased communication, education and documentation available to you 24/7.

We haven't forgotten how important it is to leave a legacy. Whether financially or through the simple gift of sharing your collection of memories, Generational Vault will house your remembrances for your loved ones when you upload pictures, videos and other important keepsakes.

BYALLACCOUNTS - Helping you stay up-to-date on your assets is an essential task as a financial services professional.

Our company stays current on your assets using a reporting technology that allows us to sync your insurance and investment assets, and deliver those account balances in an easily displayed format in your Generational Vault account. This means you have the power to access your account balances online, 24/7.

WEALTH WATCH - Helping to alert you on gains and losses from the market can be an important role for a financial services professional.

Our company uses a revolutionary system that allows us to keep an eye on your assets by using "triggers" that will automatically notify us when your account value has gone above or below the thresholds you've selected. We have the capability to monitor your entire portfolio – fixed annuities, variable annuities, 401(k)s, IRAs, ETFs, stocks, bonds, REITs and more – no matter where you are, or time of day.

RFID DATA BLOCKER CARDS - Protecting you from financial risks and pitfalls may be something you look for in a financial services professional.

Our company takes that responsibility seriously, and we believe this means protecting you from a new form of theft that uses credit card readers to scan and steal your financial information – even when your wallet is in your pocket.

When you partner with our company, you receive RFID Data Blocker Cards to protect your credit card and personal information from data skimming. These cards fit easily in your wallet and last five years.

CLIENT COMMUNICATION - Knowing that you have a financial partner is probably one of the most important responsibilities for a financial services professional to deliver.

When you partner with our company, it is our goal to maintain an active relationship with you. To best accomplish this, we rely heavily on Generational Vault to help deliver important messages and announcements to you throughout the year. It should be your destination for updated documents and educational material.

Moreover, we also recognize the value of a **face-to-face relationship**; ask us about how you can connect with us as requested or on an annual basis through Generational Vault appointment request section.

5-STAR SERVICE - Our relationship will be guided by the principles that define our organization: fiduciary, transparency and technology. We believe these hallmarks combined with our five-step New Generation Retirement Planning process will result in five-star service and a long-term partnership for your retirement success.

The hope is that by reading this book, you have gained a basic understanding of retirement income planning. If you have questions or would like support in this planning process, please contact my office:

Michael Mansfield
The Lynd Group
805-500-7035
801 South Victoria Avenue, Suite 105
Ventura, CA. 93003
Michael@TheLyndGroup.com
www.TheLyndGroup.com

ABOUT THE AUTHOR

Michael Mansfield is the owner of The Lynd Group Advisors LLC, a State Registered Investment Advisory firm in his hometown of Ventura, California. Additionally, Michael shares ownership of The Lynd Group LLC, a retirement income planning firm, with his mother Debra. Every facet of Michael's history exemplifies his passion for helping others and his natural affinity for leadership: he earned his Eagle Scout award at age 16 and later honorably served as a Cavalry Scout with the United States Army. Michael had attended Ventura College before he enlisted, continuing on with his education after his military service. He was extended an opportunity to work with a private financial planning firm while earning his Bachelor's Degree in Business Administration from Cal State San Bernardino.

It was there that he developed the passion for finance and insurance that continues to guide him. Today, Michael boasts an impressive set of financial credentials and expertise: a Certified Financial Planner™, Michael is a licensed investment advisor representative, and a former securities broker, holding his Series 66 and Series 7 license (currently inactive). Additionally, Michael is Life/Accident & Health licensed in

California. To show his true commitment to the financial profession and his clients, Michael has obtained his Master of Business Administration in Financial Planning (MBA-FP) from California Lutheran University.

For Michael, effective financial planning begins when the reality of the numbers and the needs of the individual intersect: the numbers determine the potential options, but the person sets the path. As a result, Michael is dedicated to educating his clients about the strategies and tools he suggests, not just presenting them with a product, so that they have the knowledge necessary to help them make the decision that is best suited to meet their needs. In his view, financial planners are most beneficial when they analyze the portfolio of a client and, based on their findings, develop a variety of recommendations that would provide the client with the best statistical opportunities for success. The client would then be able to select the option most closely matched to their unique needs.

Made in the USA
Columbia, SC
26 January 2019